Airbnb Business
Get your slice of the real estate pie
Without buying any property

Table of Contents

Introduction

Chapter 1 Understanding the Airbnb Platform

Chapter 2 Taking Advantage of Rental Arbitrage

Chapter 3 Airbnb vs. Vacation Rental Websites

Chapter 4 How to Create and Market Your Listing

Chapter 5 Setting the Right Price for Your Airbnb Listing

Conclusion

Introduction

In the realm of real estate investing, there is no doubt that among the most lucrative and popular investments today are rental properties. This is because they offer variety and flexibility; not to mention the high demand from both tenants and investors.

With the rapid growth of real estate investment in recent years, more and more people are enticed to invest and generate passive income. The result is more rental property options are offered on the market. One of the newest options is the Airbnb investment property.

If you are interested in investing in rental properties or renting out your idle property using the Airbnb model, this book, *Real Estate Investing through Airbnb*, will help you learn all the basics about the service.

Thanks for downloading this book, I hope you enjoy it!

Chapter 1

Understanding the Airbnb Platform

What Is Airbnb?

An online marketplace and service, Airbnb allow hosts to rent out lodging on a short-term basis. This includes shared or private rooms, apartments, vacation rentals, and homestays that typically come with basic amenities such a living room, kitchen, and heating, among others.

Airbnb provides travelers and guests with a platform to look for affordable places where they can stay in for the duration of their travel, which is often for only a short time.

The Airbnb marketplace has provided lodging to more than 17,000,000 people, connecting them with around 800,000 properties in more than 34,000 cities the world over. This is a far cry from its humble beginnings when the website could only offer one air mattress in SF, California.

With its wide international reach and unparalleled growth today, Airbnb is fast reshaping people's travel experience around the globe. It caters to a new breed of travelers who seek unique travel experiences – experiences that offer a deeper cultural immersion.

If you are considering getting into real estate investing, Airbnb offers a good way to start. It provides a good passive income stream while allowing you to help guests find suitable short-term lodging at a reasonable cost.

How Airbnb Investment Property Works

Access to an Airbnb investment property can be done in two ways: via the Airbnb official website or through the platform's mobile app. To be an Airbnb host, you must create a free account. Airbnb will charge you with 3% to 5% for each booking (guests are charged 6% to 12% as service fee).

Although Airbnb will provide recommendations on how much to charge per night, you are free to choose your rate. Guests have access to different filters to help them look for their appropriate lodging. These include dates, locations, and the number of occupants.

How to Make an Airbnb Property Investment

One thing that makes Airbnb a great platform is that you don't have to be a rental property owner to invest. All you need is a spare room in your home, rooftop, or unoccupied basement in your home to join the Airbnb investment platform.

It is important that you first study the Airbnb investment property, assess your capability as an Airbnb host, as well as the value and rates of other short-term rental properties on the market. Only when you are sure you're ready should you begin your journey as an Airbnb property investor.

Chapter 2

Taking Advantage of Rental Arbitrage

Rental Arbitrage Explained

In the context of finance, arbitrage opportunity means taking advantage of the varying rates for the same commodity. You can use this strategy to make money from Airbnb property investment. The best part is, you don't have to shell out money to buy a property to rent out. How? The rest of this chapter will discuss how you can do that.

You can sign up a long-term lease on a property for re-renting it in the short-term. You can hold the property, an apartment unit, for example, for 1 whole year. This way, you assume your landlord's risk of non-occupancy, as well as the possibility of a rental market downtrend.

By shouldering the risk, your reward is the power to ask for a higher daily rate from short-term tenants. You have a great investment opportunity if there is a considerable discrepancy between the monthly rental and the daily rental you will charge.

With the advent of the Airbnb online marketplace, opportunities like this abound. This wasn't possible during the heydays of vacation rental websites.

The Airbnb Reservations and Guest-Screening Process

Airbnb has streamlined the sub-leasing process involving reservations and guest-screening. This way, many administrative headaches have become non-existent. It has also paved the way for lower operational costs, resulting in bigger profits.

Here's an example to help you get a better idea of how it works:

Let's suppose you rent a high-end apartment in Santa Monica for $3,000/month. Similar properties cost $250/night. If you can rent out your apartment nightly for the entire month, you can have a potential rental income of $7,500 a month, or a monthly profit of $4,500.

That is easily 50 grand a year – just for one apartment. Now, imagine if you can do that for several units. Why you can leave your lucrative day job and just focus on re-renting local apartments!

Now, you may be wondering if that is even legal. Of course, there are some regulations you have to comply with, and taxes to pay. You also need permission from your landlord. But, these are only minor obstacles, and just a small price to pay for the significant passive income stream you are trying to set up. Not a lot of opportunities offer massive profits for working only a few hours each week, right?

Approaching Your Landlord about Sub-Leasing

Many Airbnb hosts today, whether or not they are aware of it, are breaking their lease agreement terms. This is because standard rental agreements don't have provisions for sub-leasing. Most property managers prefer to know who is staying in the apartment mostly for security reasons, in particular, who they will run after in case of default.

To avoid encountering problems in the future, here are some tips on how you can find cooperative landlords or property managers:

- Bigger is not necessarily better. – Talk to property managers handling smaller and fewer buildings. They are often more flexible, and more motivated to transact with long-term tenants.
- Involve your landlord or property manager. – Everyone would appreciate earning some cash on the side. You can entrust your guest check-in and key exchange procedure to the property manager in exchange for a small commission for every booking. 10% of the daily rate would be ok for the purpose.
- Professionally conduct yourself. – Use your previous experience to convince the landlord that you know what you are doing. Stunning photos of one of your existing rentals, as well as rave reviews from past

- guests, should do the trick. If the property manager sees that you maintain your unit well all year-round, he would most likely relent.
- A few white lies won't hurt. – Of course, no landlord in his right mind would agree to your plan if you bluntly tell him that you are planning to sub-lease to strangers you meet online! You can bend the truth a bit. You can tell him you're not planning to sub-lease full-time, and only for some specific instances. The key to getting your landlord's nod is to appear trustworthy and likable. It is also best to first get on his good side before attempting to ask for favors.

Chapter 3

Airbnb vs. Vacation Rental Websites

Because of the sheer number of vacation rental sites today, figuring out the best site to list your property can be tricky. Using Google to search will lead you to a massive number of specialty sites. It is also common practice for property managers to list their properties on more than 10 of these sites at a time.

The advent of the internet saw the rise of vacation rental websites. One of the pioneers, VRBO.com, started as a private rental website back in 1995. It used to rent out a solitary ski chalet. Today, the site lists more than 575,000 properties. On the other hand, Airbnb came into the picture only in 2008. After a decade, it now boasts of over 1,000,000 listed properties found in almost all countries in the world.

The vacation rental website's revenue model has remained unchanged for the past decade and a half before the arrival of Airbnb. Hosts would pay for annual subscriptions to numerous vacation rental websites. The more serious once would even pay extra for listing upgrades. This way, they would enjoy better SEO visibility.

When Airbnb entered the scene, they found a way to grab a good share of the market. They required no upfront fees, and only charged fees once bookings are confirmed.

Reasons for Airbnb's Current Market Domination

- Google-Like SEO – Airbnb makes sure that responsive hosts with rave reviews enjoy better search visibility. While most vacation rental websites feature properties for a premium fee, Airbnb utilizes an intelligent search engine in matching guests to their ideal lodging.
- Hassle-Free Transactions – Airbnb offers a simple payment process, eliminating the need for withheld deposits, obtain credit card info and process wire transfers. This simplified process allowed hosts to make same-night reservations and short-term bookings.
- One-Click Reservations – Guests can now make reservations on their own through the Instant Book option. As a host, you don't have to constantly monitor your computer to promptly respond to every incoming reservation request.
- Best Review Process – Airbnb pioneered in using the power of user feedback and social media. Because reviews are displayed prominently, hosts are under constant pressure to provide a great experience.

- Global Popularity – With users from all around the world, Airbnb easily has the widest reach.
- One-Stop Marketing Platform – With Airbnb, you don't need to employ multi-channel marketing. All you need is a well-managed single listing.
- Great User Interface – Compared to most vacation rental sites, Airbnb offers a superior map and search engine, making things more engaging to users.
- Flexibility – Airbnb caters to all types of entrepreneurs.
- Updated Calendars – As a host, you will be rewarded for actively managing your calendar, and making sure that your listed properties are available for booking.
- Quality Results – Airbnb provides your desired results, which is optimum booking.

Chapter 4

How to Create and Market Your Listing

Your goal as an Airbnb rental property investor is to come up with an impressive listing that stands out from the rest. A lot of cities have more than 10,000 Airbnb property listings. Thus, your top priority should be to get prospective guests' attention.

When browsing through volumes of properties on a listing, potential guests will rely on only 3 bits of information. Thus, it is important to provide only useful details to create a good impression and entice the user to view your property listing in full.

What You Need Do to Get Prospective Guests to View Your Listing

- The photo of your property must be high-resolution, bright, and of the right size.
- The property title must provide the location, as well as other important details.
- The picture on the profile must feature a smiling face. It must look trustworthy and likable.

Elements That Contribute to an Effective Listing

The challenge is to get more bookings for your property compared to other listed properties. Now, how do you achieve that? Simple. Make sure you use attention-grabbing headlines, punchy descriptions, beautiful pictures, and effective personal profiles.

- Use eye-catching headlines. – Drawing the right attention for your Airbnb listing using eye-catching headlines is an art form. Your headline should read something like a promise of an unforgettable experience, a sensational news story, or a well-kept secret. Imagine how you can get the reader's fancy and make him click on your listing – using only 4 – 5 words – regardless of how beautiful your picture is.

With so many other properties vying for a single user's attention, you need to be creative to win the nod of the reader, instead of your competition. If your property doesn't have anything unique or special to make it stand out, try coming up with a funny or quirky headline. When thinking of a headline, bear in mind that your primary consideration is your click-through rate. The key is to come up with a clever one-liner that would prompt a guest to click on your listing.

- Make your description precise and punchy. – Paragraph-style writing will not work in this situation. It is common for people to read the description only after the posted pictures of your property has captured their attention. Bear in mind that you only have 50 words to provide everything a prospective guest should know about the unit. These include the property's square footage, baths, and beds, among others.

A good idea is to carefully write a bulleted list that highlights the property's best-selling points. In short, what's great about your unit's amenities and location, as well as the other things that make it stand out from the rest? To give you an idea of what to include, research the competition. Then, present a list of the best features of your property.

Don't just say your unit boasts of nice stainless steel appliances. Try to be more specific. Say something like stainless steel Pro-series Frigidaire appliances. You can get ideas on what to include from websites or brochures, and other marketing materials if the building where your property is located has any.

If the listed property is yours, you can review your listing on MLS to find out what your agent discovered as your property's top features.

- Take amazing photos of your property. – There is no doubt that a listed property's most vital selling tool is its photos. More often than not, people will skip your description section altogether if they do not like what they see in the pictures you post.

Having said that, here are some things to remember when taking pictures:
- Lighting – Make sure that the rooms you feature are airy and bright. You can open as many windows as necessary to allow more light inside. Posting dull and dark photos is a sure way to drive away potential guests.
- Size of the room – If you're only using your phone to take pictures, and not using a wide-angle lens, take the shot at a high angle from one corner of the room. You must be able to cover as much area as possible to include in the photo.
- Attention to details – Include some close-up pictures of statement pieces like artwork or flower arrangements that will imply your attention to detail and style.
- Vicinity of the property – If there are amazing views or selling points in the vicinity that can help sell your property, then use them. These include the building's rooftop, gym, front lobby, or even backyard. Consider the scenarios that will help guests get a good idea of what you are offering.

Airbnb offers free photography services in case you are not confident in your ability to take high-quality pictures and scenes. It is also important to make sure that the major furnishings and interior design layout are done before scheduling a viewing appointment. Whenever necessary, retake new pictures to update those you have previously posted. This may be necessary when you change furniture or décor.

Hiring a professional photographer to take pictures of your property is a sound idea. But, if you want to do it on your own, you should use a wide-angle lens. Try to come up with professional-looking photos in terms of color and lighting. Using a GoPro is an affordable and easy way to get amazing wide-angle options from a basic camera.

- Add pictures to your listing. – It is important to be mindful of the order of adding pictures. Remember that Airbnb only allows uploading of 3 primary pictures. The first picture is often the attention-grabber. Ideally, it should feature the unit's roomiest room or a one of a kind outdoor space. The search results will display the picture. Thus, you need to be careful when deciding which picture to upload.

Feature the master bedroom in your second photo, while it is up to you to decide what to use for your 3rd picture. But, it must be as unique as possible. it must be something that you think will help make the property stand out from its competitors.

The rest of your pictures must be shown in such a way that will help your guests have a good idea of your property's layout. Put yourself in the prospective guest's place. Imagine you are walking through the front door, what do you like to see? Then, take photos of the first room you enter.

While Airbnb does not allow videos at present, you must organize your photos to appear similar to a walk-through video. You don't need to take different pictures of the same room – even if they are taken from various angles. The saying that less is more applies here.

Try to limit your pictures to around 12. This is because some wireless connections and websites can be quite slow or slow-loading. Avoid taking excessive photos of plants, artwork, and another décor, unless they are really special.

You may have some stuff in your home that you consider exciting a special such as an impressive pottery collection. For most people, this is not a factor when choosing a place to rent. So, why even bother to include them?

Chapter 5

Setting the Right Price for Your Airbnb Listing

A lot of inexperienced rental property investors is to set the wrong price for their property. It's either too high (unaffordable) or too low (unprofitable).

A good place to start is your monthly mortgage or rent payment for the property. Divide it by 30 to come up with a rough estimate of your monthly cost. While this may not be an accurate way to price your property, it will at least give you a ballpark figure.

Here's a more scientific approach:

- Check out your competition. – Whether you like it or not, you are competing not only with other Airbnb property listings in the area but also with hotels and hostels. Your eye-catching photos and awesome descriptions would not be of much help if you don't have competitive pricing.

To give you a good idea of how much your property is worth, check out how much other similar properties in the area are going for. Your pricing goal is to stay within the same range as the other similar listings in the area.

- Do you have add-ons and perks? – You can charge a bit more if you offer some amenities that other listings don't. For example, your

- listing comes with fancy linens, cable or a washer & dryer. You may also offer a free bottle of wine or fruit basket for each stay. If your guests have access to a specific parking space or extra garage storage, don't hesitate to charge more. The logic is, these things would cost your guests extra if they aren't included in your package.
- Start low, but aim high. – Initially, your focus should be to get your first guest, and a first rave review. This may mean lowering your rates to undercut your competition.

While some people do not mind spending more, a lot of potential guests will go for the most affordable accommodations possible. If other similar listings are going for $100 a night, try offering your place at $75 just to see how it will fare. Once your bookings start to pick up, you can adjust your rates based on the market demands.

- Set your limits. – A good thing about Airbnb is that it is a self-governing ecosystem. This means the price is determined by supply and demand. It is a win-win situation if, after raising your rates, people still come to you. On the other hand, if you raised your prices beyond the market, you just have to lower it.
- Set pricing for holidays and special events. – It's alright to adjust your rates for holidays, weekends, and special events. Hotels do it all the time.

You can easily do this using Airbnb's advanced pricing calendar and pricing tool.
- Set up a security deposit policy. – You can ask for a security deposit as insurance in case anything goes awry. Although Airbnb already includes insurance, a security deposit will cover you for minor issues like lost kitchen appliances, scratched floors, or broken dishes.
- Charge a fee for cleaning. – Cleaning requires money, energy, and time – whether it is done through a cleaning service, a maid, or yourself. How much to charge will depend on the size of the place? The service includes mopping, vacuuming, cleaning the sheets, and tidying up the kitchen, among others.
- Charge a fee for extra guests. – Airbnb allows charging extra for additional guests. Your listing may be ideal for only 2 guests, but an extra guest or 2 may be allowed for an additional nightly fee. The extra charge can be justified since more occupants mean more mess.

The bottom line is, you must set a rate that you are comfortable asking. If you were the guest, would you be comfortable paying it? Make sure that the price already includes cleaning and other extra work needed.

Conclusion

I'd like to thank you and congratulate you for transiting my lines from start to finish.

I hope this book was able to help you to gain a better understanding of Airbnb property investing.

The next step is to use the tips and strategies provided in this book.

I wish you the best of luck

www.ingramcontent.com/pod-product-compliance
Lightning Source LLC
Chambersburg PA
CBHW031942170526
45157CB00008B/3273